Lingerie

text ANNA FOLLI

edited by VALERIA MANFERTO DE FABIANIS
editorial coordination GIADA FRANCIA
graphic design MARINELLA DEBERNARDI

Con/tents

10 Introduction

16 The Corset: A History of Imprisonment

50 Rehearsals for Seduction in a Poster

114 And the Stars Strip Off …

186 Angels on the Catwalk

254 Photo credits

Introduction

Once upon a time in the Garden of Eden, Adam and Eve lived unclothed. Then, one day, they ate of the apple of sin and felt the need to cover themselves with a fig leaf. Perhaps lingerie was born at that moment, the product of need and desire. But what makes a woman wear an item of underwear? Is it modesty or the desire to please? Probably both. It is the wish to accentuate an intimate part of one's body.

Over time, shoulders, breasts, waist, bottom and even ankles have been hidden, adorned or compressed according to the ideal of femininity of the time.

Women have been imprisoned in corsets reinforced by whalebone, bound within knickers with laces and very uncomfortable garters. But now women wear garments which are as light as a feather – and which caress the skin when they touch it.

The history of lingerie runs parallel to that of the emancipation of women. An imaginary gallery of shirts, crinolines, corsets, girdles, silk stockings and knickers of every shape, cut and color reveal the passage of time from the years of punishment to those of seduction. And they illustrate women's long journey from the demure dimension of the housewife to the more blatantly erotic reaches of the imagination. Women change: they squeeze in their waists and breasts to resemble androgynous models, or they transform themselves into curvaceous sirens. For every change in taste, there suddenly appears a flimsy and seductive babydoll, or a bra which embraces and supports, an underslip which reveals more than it conceals. Gone are the days when lingerie was only white, black or, at most, flesh colored: today female underwear can be found in all the colors of the rainbow. Often, it is not just a plain color but striped or decorated with hearts, stars and a host of enchanting patterns. According to taste and the occasion, functional or precious fabrics are used: lace, fish-net, voile, silk, rayon, cotton. There is also a choice between strings, velcro or hooks. Underwear is now a protagonist and can no longer be hidden away modestly; it peeps out of the neckline of a shirt or low-cut jeans.

A quick digression into the history of lingerie reveals unsuspected connections with the evolution of customs. One can start as early as the 2nd millennium B.C. when the women of Crete had a role of great importance. And it was highlighted by the fact that they kept their breasts bare and wore a small corset which exalted their femininity. In the 1st century B.C. a small strip of cloth called the *apodesmo*, which supported the bust so it did not swing when a women was walking, is very revealing about the classical ideals of beauty in the Greek world. In the Dark Ages, after the fall of the Roman Empire, even the chest was hidden and compressed by bindings and bandages.

The Middle Ages conferred a particular, rather disturbing, importance on the ankles, which were concealed in an austere fashion by long garments and even longer trains. In the 15th century, when a woman's greatest endowment was fertility, noble women accentuated their rounded stomachs by introducing padding under their skirts. In time corsets, crinolines, underskirts, robes became so elegant that they were worthy of being shown rather than hidden. The first bra was seen on the eve of the First World War. It was invented by the Cadolle company, founded in 1887 in Buenos Aires but which later moved to

Paris where it had an exceptional clientèle: one customer was Mata Hari who had bras made with special secret pockets. A countess wanted them made with gold hooks which were supplied specially by Cartier. Christina Onassis bought all the collections in every color range available and had each model sent to all of her six homes.

In every period, underwear is conceived differently: at the end of the Renaissance to be fashionable a woman had to demonstrate that she was virtuous, while in the 17th century she had to be a libertine. And what about today? Great freedom of choice, naturally. But without ever losing the dream – and making others dream too.

1 A sinful detail from the *guepière* designed by Lolita Lempicka for the '98/'99 Fashion Show.

4-5 A group of women, busy dressing mannequins in a Portsmouth corset factory in 1938.

7 Penelope Cruz radiates sensuality in a scene from the musical *Nine*.

8 Heidi Klum on the catwalk for Victoria's Secret.

15 The corset: from a method of constriction to an instrument of seduction.

The Corset: A History of Imprisonment

The Corset: A History of Imprisonment

In Fall 1795, during a ball at the Opéra, Madame Tallien, the undisputed queen of Parisian fashion, appeared before her delighted admirers wearing a silk tunic under which she was wearing no underwear. There was no corset to enhance her perfect shape. "I don't need it" – she claimed – "I only need to bathe in strawberry and raspberry juice to look my best." There may be some doubts about the effectiveness of this elixir of beauty. However, in a period when the corset was an absolutely essential garment in every woman's wardrobe, refusing to wear one was sufficient for Madame Tallien to be considered a revolutionary spirit. The crowning glory of female lingerie, the corset is much more than a simple item of underwear and has always been considered the most seductive of garments. And there is no wonder: any woman squeezed into a rigid little corset with strings and laces becomes a seductive *femme fatale*. For this reason, even though the corset was, in many cases, a real prison which could cause terrible damage, for many years women were unable to discard it. There are tales of inexplicable deaths of young noble ladies, caused by broken ribs which perforated the lungs.

In less serious cases, corsets which were too tight, prevented breathing and caused continuous fainting in the unfortunate wearers. Enlightened doctors and the social philosopher Jean-Jacques Rousseau condemned these dangerous "body squeezers." But to no avail.

The corset had been created in Renaissance times to model the female body and adapt it to the rules of the period: squeeze in the waist, support and accentuate the bust (or on the contrary, reduce its dimension by flattening it); shaping and sometimes highlighting the hips. But very soon it also took on the very precise significance of social superiority. Squeezed and elegantly dressed, indeed women were unable to do any work and, in order to wear it, they needed domestic help.

Furthermore, the fact that a woman's body, wrapped in corsets and crinolines, buried under layers of frills, skirts and underskirts, appeared completely unnatural, rendered it even more seductive and desirable. It did not matter if sometimes the complications of elaborate mechanisms made corsets look more like orthopedic contraptions rather than instruments of seduction. In the 19th century, with the need to have wasp waists and breathtakingly low necklines, the fashion for corsets underwent an absolute explosion. There were types of all shapes and sizes: ball and wedding corsets, morning and night corsets, corsets for travel, riding, singing, dancing, swimming. Corsets in damask, satin, brocade, suede, Valenciennes lace, or crocheted with silk thread. And even perfumed with little bags of lavender sewn in the center. The first advertising campaign for the sale of underwear appeared in the shop window of a corset maker who boasted about the quality of his latest model: "Restrains large breasts, supports weak ones and holds sagging ones together." And so, how do you manage without one? Even in the new millennium the basque, as it is called today, had a new revival and became an important part of underwear. Extremely feminine and sexy for the evening, more sporty and casual during the day, the post-modern version of the corset is still a source of inspiration for the most intimate of male fantasies.

19 On the Boulevard de Strasbourg in Paris, in 1926, an entire shop window full of corsets of all styles and fashion.

20-21 A young lady poses as model for corsets in an illustration from 1890.

1770-80

An English corset created between 1770 and 1780. Made out of a red wool material, it is decorated with cream-colored linen trim and embroidery.

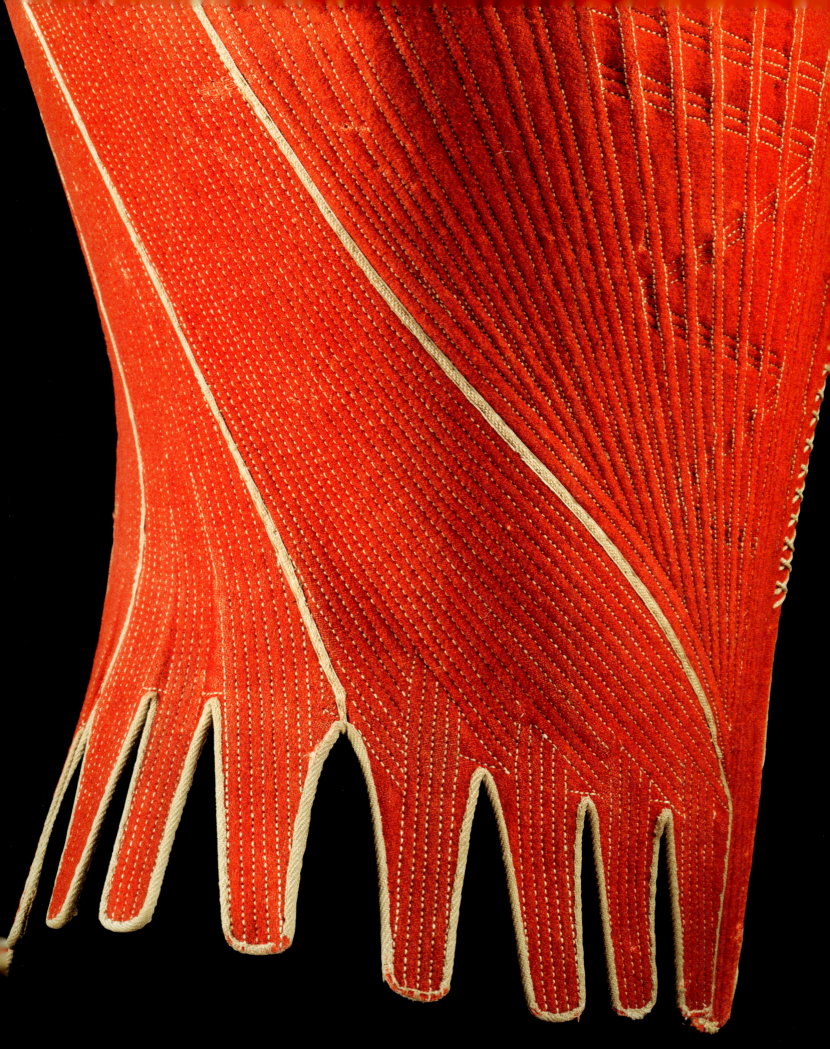

1780-90

A linen-and-silk corset made in Great Britain between 1780 and 1790.
The picture spotlights the high quality of the finishings on the back.

1770-90

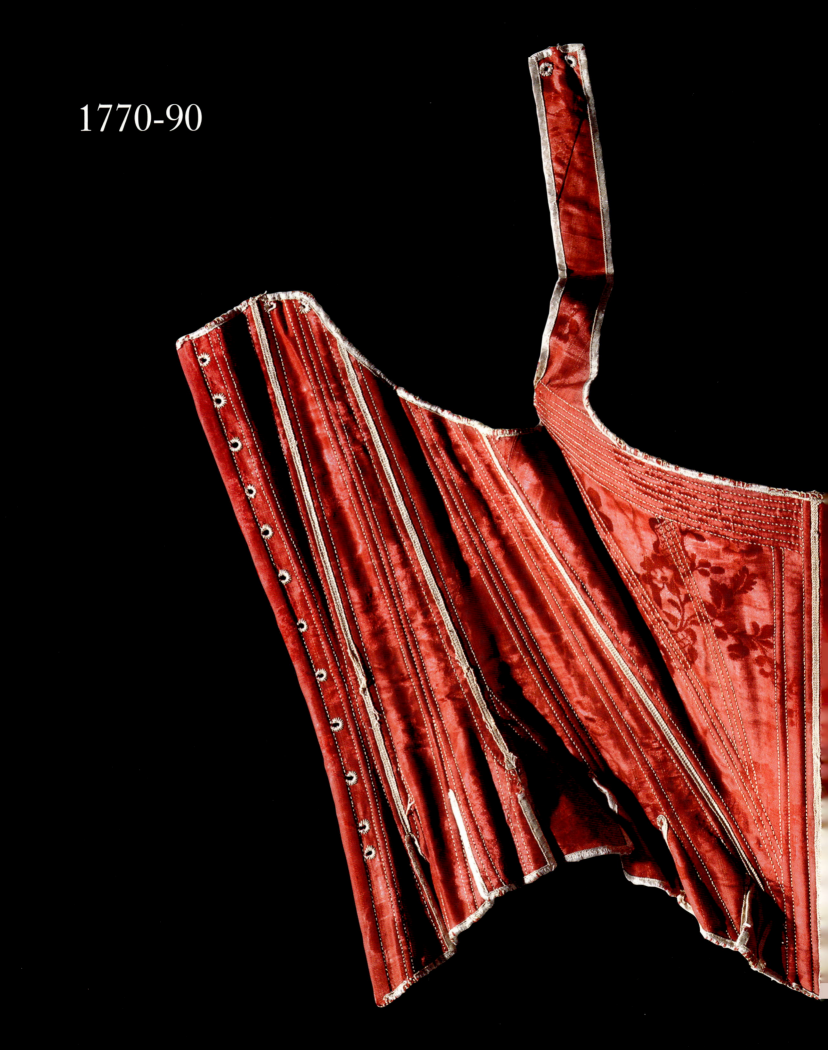

A precious whalebone girdle. It was made in Great Britain using high-quality materials: damask, silk and linen.

1851

In 1851, this corset was designed for minimal constriction of the female body, though it could still reduce waistlines by up to 20 inches (50cm).

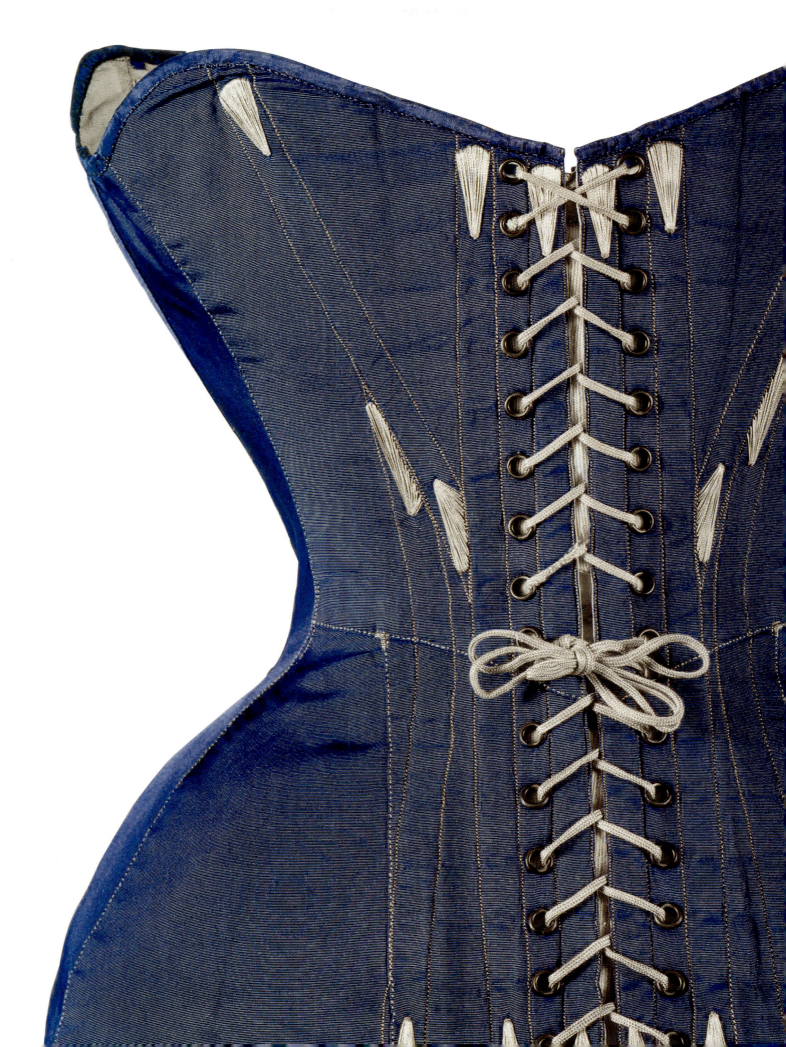

1887

A corset made by English craftsman Edwin Izod.
It is made of satin with lace trim.

1870-90

A whalebone silk corset. This model used to be made in France and Great Britain.

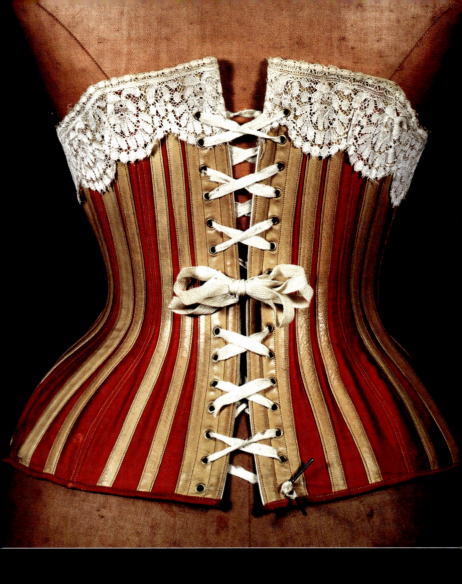

1870-90

An English corset of the 1880s.
It was made of red satin with yellow leather trimmings.

1880-90

The sumptuous and elegant detailing on a late 19th-century corset stands out against the shiny bronze silk.

1890

A French red satin corset decorated with a black lace trim.

42-43 A corset made by Airtex in London around 1890. It is made of cotton with a *broderie anglaise* trim.

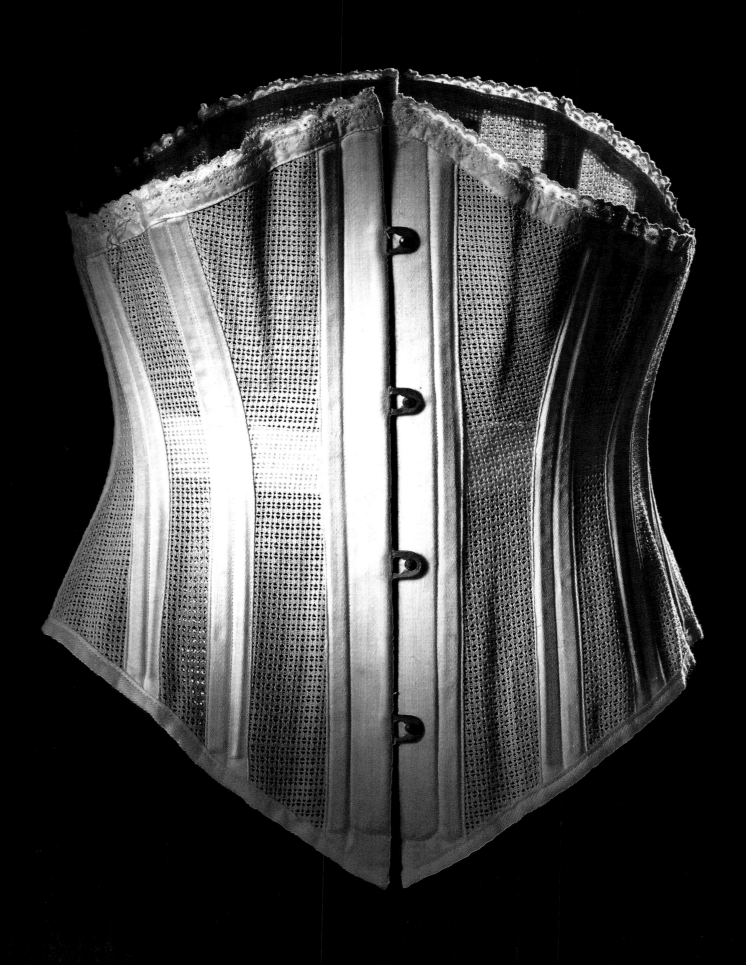

1890

This particular corset was made with ribbons and whalebone sticks, which helped to achieve the desired silhouette.

1890

A very particular corset made out of silk ribbons.
Very probably of English manufacture.

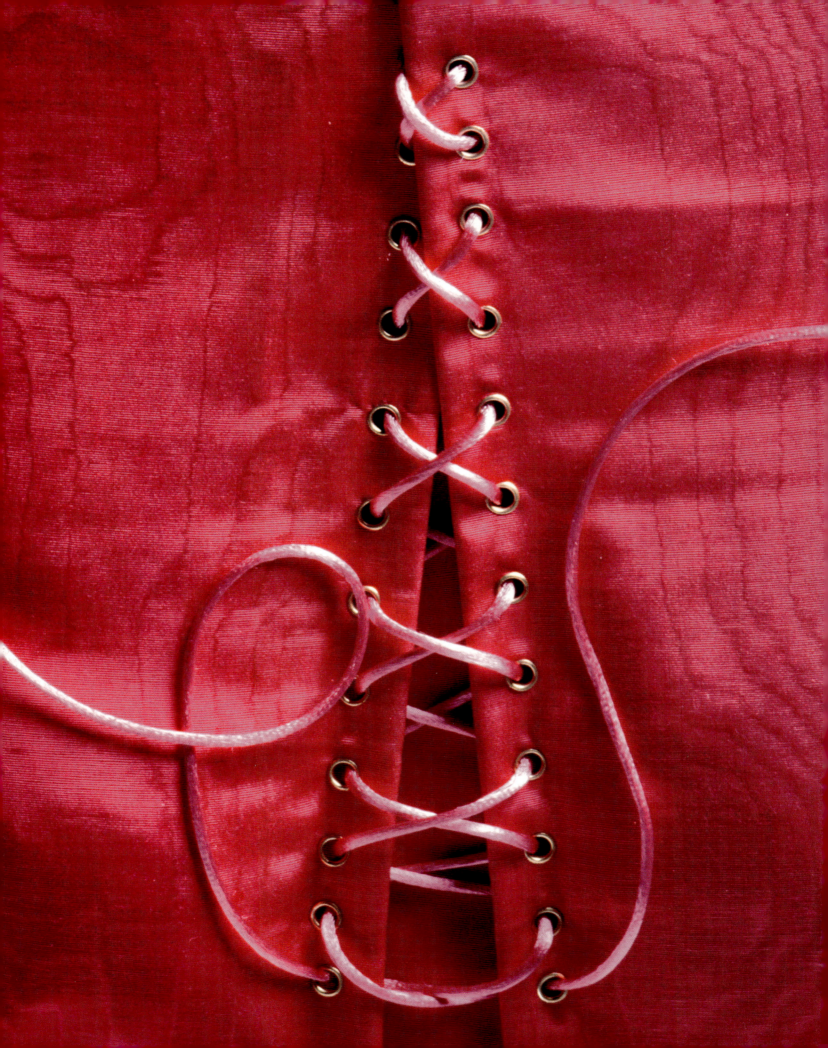

Detail from a late 19th-century corset, highlighting the fastening with metal eyelets and silk ribbons.

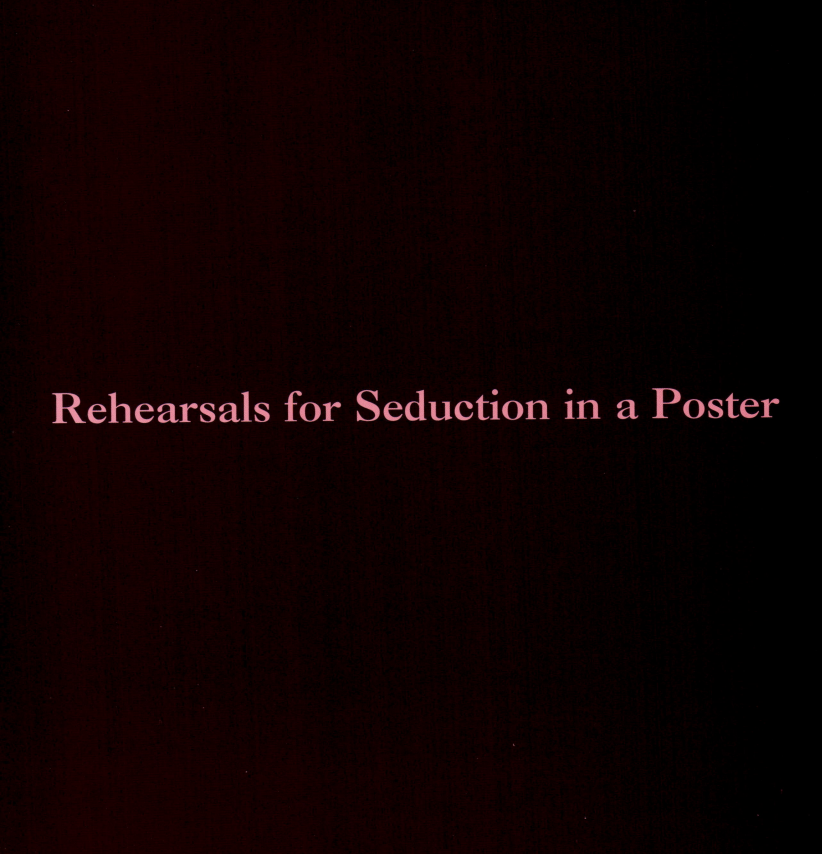
Rehearsals for Seduction in a Poster

Rehearsals for Seduction in a Poster

In an advertising poster of 1870, a group of women with their bodies clad in seductive lingerie, is featured in very refined drawings which hint but do not reveal. In another poster, the female silhouette takes on the appearance of a blooming flower. In a third, the tendency to explain prevails over the desire to seduce: what counts is to demonstrate the utility of a particularly enveloping and constricting corset. But there are also those among the pioneers in lingerie advertising who are capable of resorting to the instrument of irony, showing in a cartoon the difference between those who use and those who do not use the right lingerie.

What are the strategies used to advertise an item of lingerie? Indeed many, obviously varying according to the times and the company selling it. Take a look at the first advertising posters from the second half of the 19th century. You only have to look at them to understand the evolution of taste and femininity over the last fifty years. The real revolution exploded from the 1970s onwards. Women were emancipated. Women were no longer female enchantresses or guardians of the domestic hearth: comfort and convenience were important for women.

And status was equally important. And to reach it,
advertising explained that it is essential to start from
lingerie...

A well- researched campaign can reinforce and stimulate these needs. It is important to have a different strategy depending on whether the product is aimed at a mass market or at an élite market. In the former case wide-audience media are chosen, often even television, and simple slogans which are easy to remember, such as "For every woman. . . ." series, used successfully by Triumph. Or you exploit the fame of models and actresses. Playtex is one of the first companies in the sector to use product endorsement. It was Eva Herzigova who wore the famous Wonderbra which was immediately renamed "the miracle bra."

To address an élite, there was a preference for artistic pictures taken by famous photographers and published in a few select magazines. The concept of "exclusivity" in these cases is considered decisive.

A symbolic case is that of la Perla which has always concentrated its efforts on being precious, so much so that even a pair of knickers is worn like a jewel.

But not all strategies are winning strategies, There are cases where advertising ran the risk of having negative effects. This happened with the Mitoufle company which was the first, in France, to sell tights and advertise them with an innovative campaign. What had not been anticipated however, was that by then most women already knew about tights and started to buy the cheaper ones manufactured by Dim.

An example of a successful advertising strategy, on the other hand, is that of Playtex, with its "Criss Cross" model which for years topped the sales figures. The clever slogan "the bra with the magic cross" contributed to the success of a product which sold 800,000 units per year.

A real record. And today? Nowadays, we tend to concentrate on the brand rather than on the model. The stronger the image of a company, the easier it becomes to sell its products. And demonstrating this in a rather forceful way there is the "case" of Victoria's Secret...

53 This ad poster was designed by Leo Kline in 1937 to promote a Kestos Lingerie bra, recommended for both day use as well as evening wear.

56-57 This refined illustration was published together with an article on female lingerie in *La Vie Parisienne* in 1870.

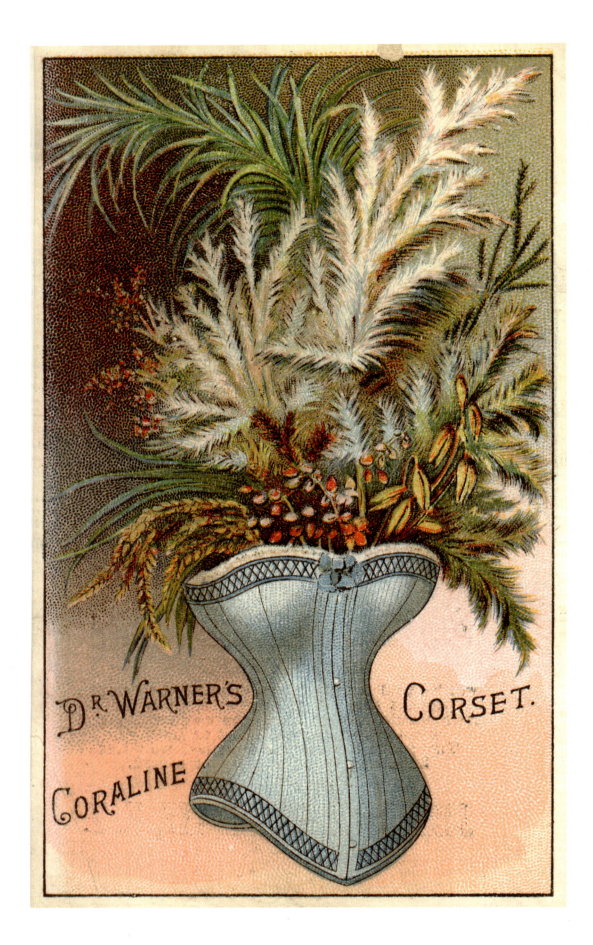

A corset with leaves and flowers coming out of it: Art Deco in full swing, this image fully reflects the tastes of the times.

1880

1880

Delicate and flowery, this is the picture chosen by Dr. Warner's Corset Co. to advertise its product.

60 Queen Bess corsets and underskirts are advertised in this flier, which appeared in England in 1880.

61 An ad poster of the English company "Harness' Electric Corsets" recommends its corsets to women of all ages.

62-63 Workers in a Chinese laundry are busy washing old and new corsets. The ad dates back to 1885.

SIDE & DRESS STEELS.

WARRANTED NOT TO RUST.

WITH THE NEW CELLULOID CLASPS IN

CHAS. SHIELDS SONS 20 & 22 GOLD ST. N.Y

1894

An ad poster by Charles Martene for the Hairdressing Exhibition.

1897

A poster by Gaston Noury for "Les Corsets Le Furet."

1895

et après la cure.

The ad poster for a new slimming therapy in France in 1895.

1901

This poster of the famous corset company, Le Furet, reflects the style precepts of Art Nouveau in the sinuous elegance of the female shape.

70-71 An elegant 1907 poster advertises "Aux Corsets Merveilleux," one of the best producers of corsets in Paris.

...s Merveilleux

Maison BAEHR & Cie
Inventeurs du CORSET L'EXPANSIBLE

MAISON DE CONFIANCE FONDÉE EN 1882

66, Chaussée-d'Antin, Paris

La plus grande spécialité de Corsets de Paris

EXPOSITION UNIVERSELLE 1900
Membre du Jury — Hors Concours

SE MÉFIER DES CONTREFAÇONS

La Maison n'a aucune Succursale

(A.D.)

Téléphone 108.57

72 This "Warner's Rust Proof Corset" poster, dates back to 1909.

73 An ad poster produced for "Spécialité Corset." The poster announces a "Corset Ball," to be held on the January 28, 1902 at the Continental Hotel in Paris.

LA PREMIÈRE POSE

— Vraiment, pour faire mon portrait, il est nécessaire que je me déshabille ?

74 It is only 1919 but "the Lady in her underslip" with her mischievous style reflects the new desire to transgress.

75 In a 1928 poster, an elegant lady dressed in pink with high heels shows off a delightful pair of culottes.

76 and 77 Changing times . . . The ladies in these two pictures show the comfort afforded by "Ceinture Roussel" corsets, modern elastic corsets that, going only as far down as the waist, ensure both support and freedom of movement.

LE SOUTIEN-GORGE MADOR

78 In Mador's 1930 ad poster, the picture of a young woman evokes a feeling of freedom.

79 With a stylized and evanescent picture this poster advertises every woman's dream: Furet Corsets.

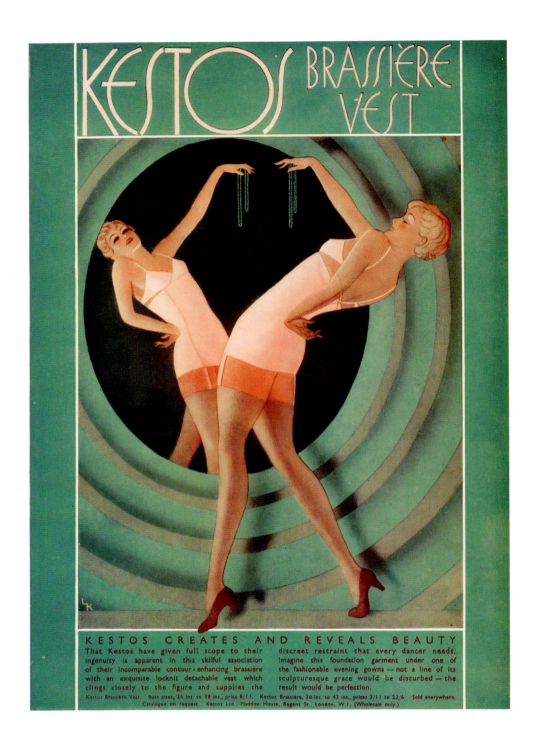

Two 1932 posters advertising "Kestos Lingerie." Corsets and whalebone had disappeared by then and the new pictures suggest youth, cheerfulness and freedom of movement.

KESTOS BRASSIÈRE & ZOMA BELT

KESTOS CREATES AND REVEALS BEAUTY

Pour le sport... for dancing... for all occasions where comfort and freedom must be considered, yet smartness is essential, the Kestos Brassière, with its scientific crossway pull, which provides uplift without the least restriction and delicately accentuates feminine contours, is indispensable. In the subtleties of its design can be found "perfect beauty," yet it is simplicity itself to adjust, and light and comfortable to wear. With the Zoma Belt, a masterpiece of practical efficiency, ingeniously designed to maintain an even tension on the stockings and remain firmly in position under all circumstances, the most ardent sportswoman can indulge in her favourite pastimes unhampered by any discomfort or restriction of movement.

Kestos Zoma Belt, prices 4/11, 9/11. Kestos Brassière, 30 ins. to 42 ins., prices from 3/11 to 22/6. Sold everywhere. Catalogue on request. Kestos Ltd., Maddox House, Regent Street, London, W.1. (Wholesale only.)

An elegant selection of women's underwear: from nightdresses with a bolero, to silk underslips; from a set with lace inserts to a long dressing gown.

1932

—and Loveliness

What more charming than this Empire nightdress, with its gathered top and straight back caught in with a sash. The uncommon cream lace bolero is separate. Very pretty and simple with its crossover lace trimming is this strap cami-knicker model of lily green triple ninon. The next model is cut with knickers and a brassière top. Make this of washing satin and inset lace medallions. A very slim-fitting design is this last, and so, too, is the princess slip you see sketched folded. This has a deep lace insertion, and the top is cut brassière fashion. The dressing-gown needs no introduction. It is the style we all like, made in patterned silk quilting, which is something fresh.

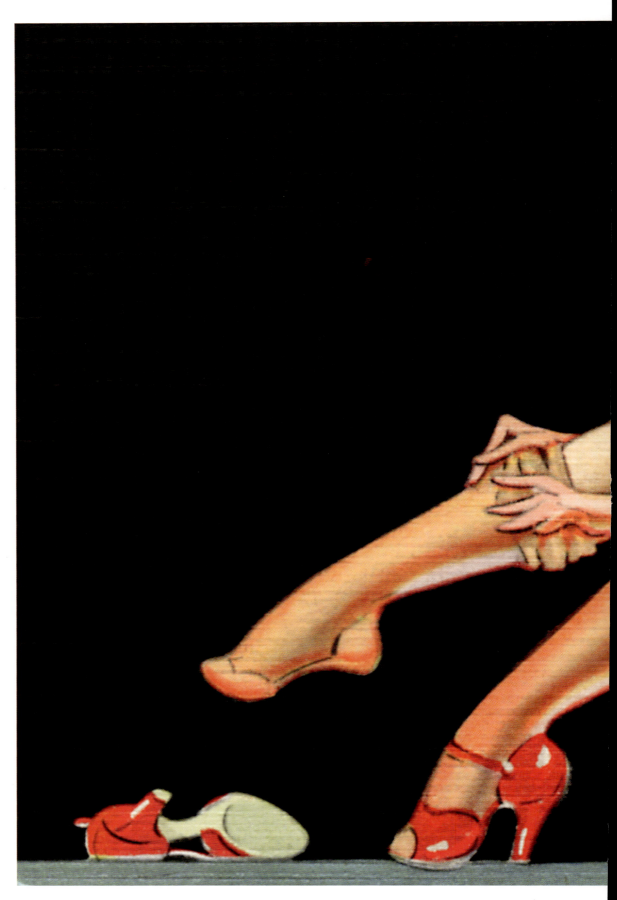

1940

A decisively provocative postcard. An attractive girl wearing an underslip and garters invites her lover to write to her. . .

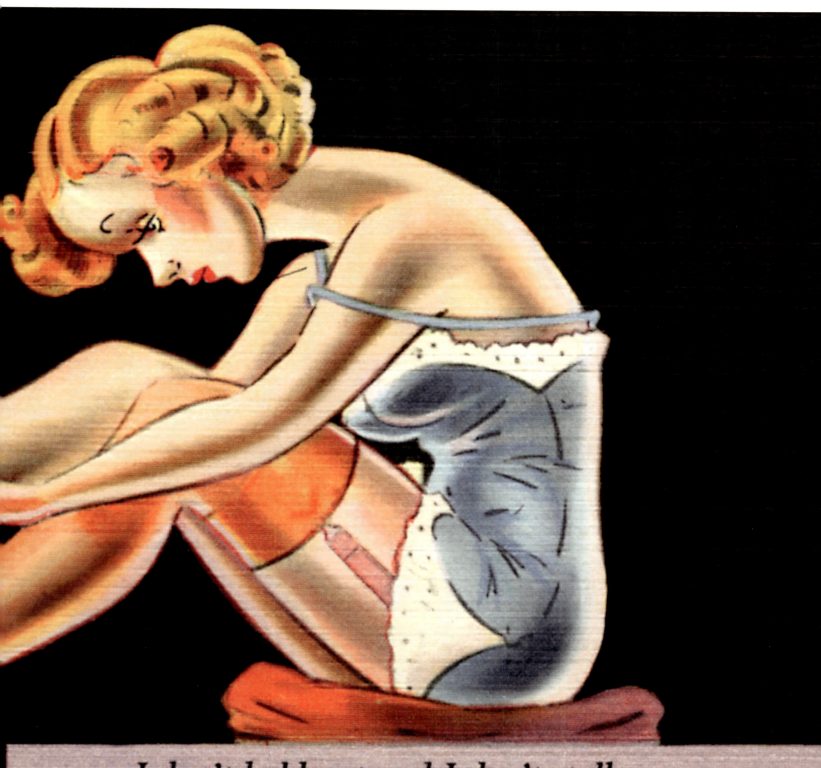

1949

Ad posters become more and more provocative.
In this picture that was created for Emo, a luxury lingerie company,
a young woman is wearing stockings . . . but nothing else.

1950

The image of a woman transformed. In this ad for Maidenform Bra, the protagonist is portrayed as a pistol-wielding bandit.

I dreamed I was

WANTED
in my Maidenform* bra

'FRAME-UP'* new bra with 3-way support
Embroidered panels frame, outline and separate the cups. Extra-firm supports at the sides give you extra uplift. Stretch band at the bottom keeps the bra snug and securely in place. It's a 'Frame-up'—in A, B, C cups.

IT'S A STEAL, AT $1.59

*REG. U.S. PAT. OFF. ©1963 BY MAIDENFORM, INC., MAKERS OF BRAS, GIRDLES, SWIMSUITS

Good-bye "Bulging Tummy"

Thanks to the wonderful new girdle that holds you flat as a pancake!

the fabulous **Nite-'n-Day** GIRDLES · PANTIES

Figure needs streamlining? Here's an easy way to get that trim, *flat tummy* you need to do justice to your clothes.

The secret? Just slip into a Nite-'n-Day, the marvelous new girdle that's "nature-cut." It gently curves and molds you in three strategic places—holds you flat as a pancake *comfortably*, with never a *trace* of a bulge!

Buy the girdle or the pantie (or both!)... in fabrics as sleek and luxurious as your best lingerie. And we've priced it to fit young budgets. Small (24"-25" waist), medium (26", 27", 28" waist), large (29"-30" waist); in frosted white or peppermint pink.

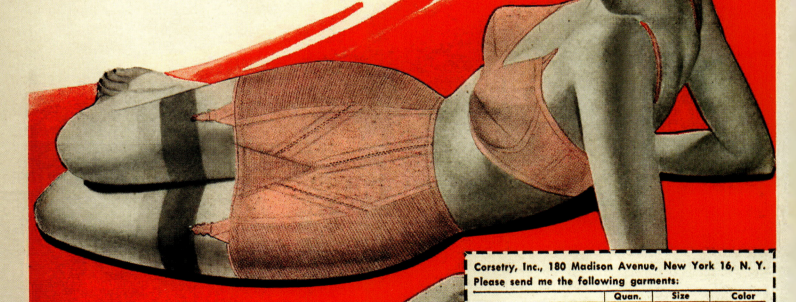

STYLE No. 100— **GIRDLE** $5.95
STYLE No. 101—PANTIE— $6.50

Priced slightly higher west of the Rockies.
At better stores everywhere. If your favorite store or shop doesn't have your size, use mail-order coupon below. For your convenience, your order will be filled through the store nearest you.

Corsetry, Inc., 180 Madison Avenue, New York 16, N. Y.
Please send me the following garments:

	Quan.	Size	Color
No. 100—Girdle at $5.95			
No. 101—Pantie at $6.50			

NAME
ADDRESS
CITY _____ ZONE _____ STATE _____
☐ Money Order   ☐ Check   ☐ C.O.D.
(If delivered in New York City, add 2% Sales Tax)

1950

In the Fifties, women's underwear underwent a real revolution. Above all, underwear was expected to be practical – the aspect highlighted in these pictures published in the most important women's magazines.

It's paradise!

FLOATING ACTION
with tension-free tangent straps!

For a thrilling new outlook, you need the gentle beauty-lift of a Floating Action bra. The fabulous tangent straps hold up the whole bra (not just the cups!) because they're cleverly anchored at the sides. That's why you never have a whit of strain on bosom or shoulder. That's why your rounded uplifted curves stay up, even when you whirl, twirl, bend or stretch.

Style 372, superfine poplin, A, B & C cups. **18/-**.
Style 376, nylon, **22/-**.

Now! LONG LINE Floating Action

For perfect figure control, comfort and glamour! Style 592, superfine poplin, B cup 34-42, C cup 34-44, **27/-**.

THE BRA THAT'S A BEAUTY TREATMENT

At your favourite store, or write to Dept. 104, Exquisite Form Brassiere (G.B.) Ltd.

1955

The unique, unmistakable style of celebrated fashion illustrator René Gruau lent a touch of sensual elegance to advertisements for Lejaby and Jacques Fath lingerie.

1954

In the Fifties, women were still viewed as feminine; gentle and reassuring. They were supposed to have a slim waistline and a large bust, as in this ad for Maidenform Bras.

1958

In this ad for Lou, it is the doctor who suggests which bra model to wear.

Why wear anything else?

'Taj Mahal' and 'Butterfly'. Two new ranges in Bri-Nylon
from Warners, where the new ideas come from.
So pretty it would be a shame to wear anything else.

Warners

1960

Apart from color, in the Sixties, lingerie acquired new patterns and a wider range of models. Depending on a woman's physique, taste and requirements, she could choose styles of knickers of reduced or bigger dimensions.

1970

In the Seventies, the watchword was "freedom of choice." The caption in Triumph's ad page reads: "Triumph has the bra that is right for you." According to your taste, you could opt for a leopardskin model or for a simple white one.

1980

For every moment of the day, there is the right bra. There are special models for sportswomen, with cups that give increased support.

102-103 1994 is the year that saw the birth of the Wonderbra: the bra which makes any woman look well endowed. The new product met with outstanding success – and beautiful model, Eva Herzigova, who was chosen for the ad, contributing toward this unexpected success.

104 and 105 For year 2000, famous underwear manufacturers like Triumph updated their ad language, combining a traditional image with a surprising virtual model.

106 La Perla lingerie has become synonymous with exclusivity because it is so elegant and precious.

107 Over the last few years, famous designers like Armani have started to produce refined items of underwear.

108-109 Among the models chosen to endorse Victoria's Secret is the seductive Laetitia Casta, wearing the Whiteley model.

The way you are changes all the time. It reflects in what you do, when and where. But however you're feeling, Triumph has the bra for the way you are.

Soft, stretchy, natural-looking bras that look great under T-shirts.

Delicate, lacy and underwired bras, so beautiful they're almost too good to cover up.

Cool and comfortable bras that move, bend and stretch when you do...perfect for good sports.

Whichever Triumph bra you choose, you'll find it shapes up to your lifestyle. Beautifully.

Photography: Roger Charity.
Lycra® is the registered trademark for DuPont's elastane fibre

OR ARE YOU JUST PLEASED TO SEE ME?

THE PUSH-UP BALCONETTE BRA. AVAILABLE IN SIZES 32-36A AND 32-38BC.

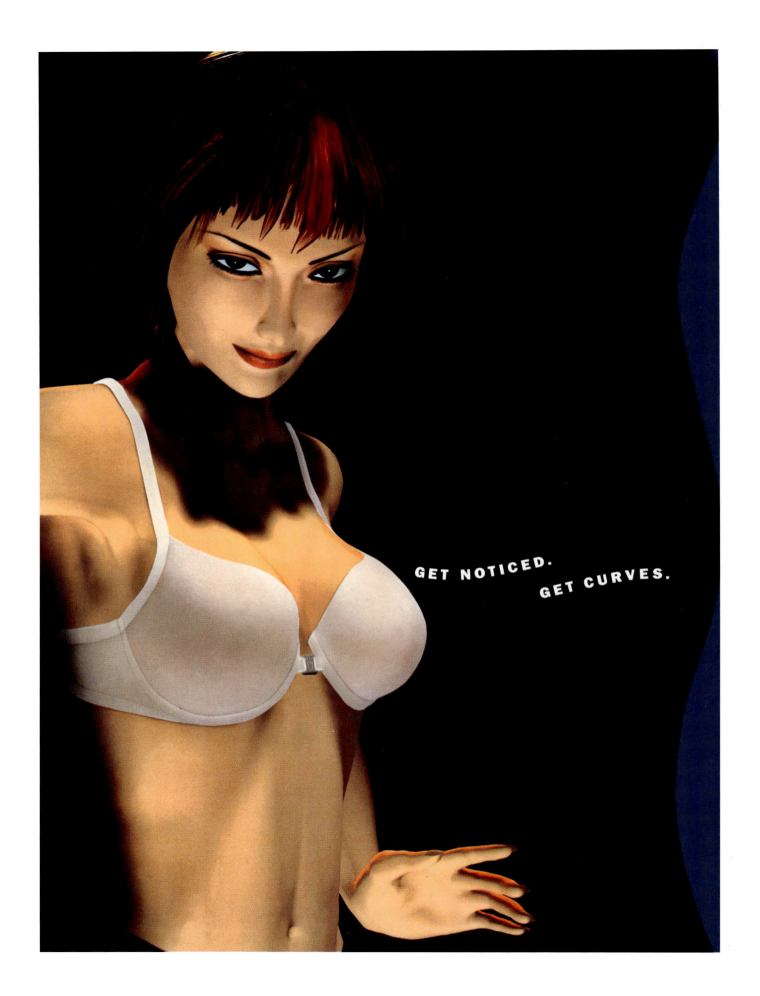

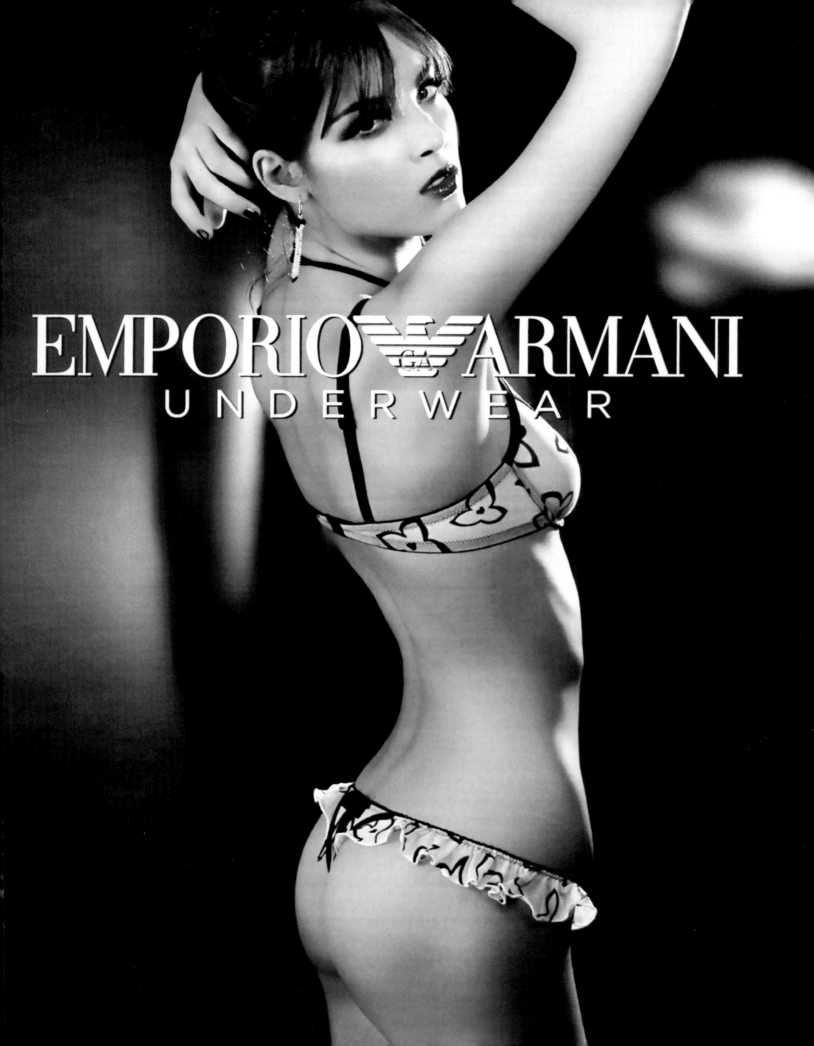

On 23 September 2008, at the presentation of the new Wonderbra collection, Dita von Teese posed sitting on a giant bra.

2008

And the Stars Strip Off …

And the Stars Strip Off …

Silhouetted by a simple white satin underslip. Or wrapped in a lace robe which reveals more than it hides. Sexier than ever, in a seductive black corset. Nobody more potently than Marilyn Monroe has demonstrated the disturbing power of a simple lingerie garment. She loved being photographed wearing mischievous baby-doll pajamas which exalted the beauty of her body. And what can we say about Billy Wilder's film *The Seven Year Itch*, in which Marilyn devised a system to deal with the oppressive heat by putting her bra in the fridge, making her innumerable admirers "shudder."

But Monroe was not the only star who knew how to exploit the power of lingerie. It is impossible to forget Marlene Dietrich's black stockings, Carole Lombard's comfortable and refined pajamas, Elizabeth Taylor's silk underslips. In the Fifties, it was actresses who transformed the underslip into an osé garment: provocative enough to arouse male fantasies, the underslip is not immodest enough to upset censorship regulations. And it was also film stars who made the underslip fashionable again after it had been considered unfashionable for years. With its flared shape, it was perfect for highlighting a slim waist and an ample bust, as dictated by the fashion precepts of the time.

There has always been a very close relationship between lingerie and actresses.

The forerunner of fashion for curvaceous women was American actress, Mae West, the first sex symbol in the history of cinema. In the respectable and puritan America of the 1930s, she became the subject of a witch hunt and she was accused of showing off her curves with excessively provocative lingerie.

As far as shapeliness is concerned, Jane Russell was no less deserving as she was better known for her bosom than her acting abilities. In order to keep her bosom under control, during the filming of his "first" film *The Outlaw*, producer Howard Hughes resorted to his expertise in aerodynamic to invent a special bra which was more like armor than lingerie.

The low-necklines of Jane Russell, Anita Ekberg, Jane Mansfield and Sophia Loren were equally famous, wearing bras which were specially made to lift and enhance the bust.

The corset made a triumphant return thanks to the most creative star of our time.

In her European tour in 1990, Madonna wore a very unusual flesh-colored corset with exaggeratedly pointed cups, causing a rush to buy this long-forgotten garment. Nicole Kidman had a similar effect when, in *Moulin Rouge*, she wore a corset and suspenders in an enchantingly retro style.

We must not forget the undeniable erotic power of Kim Basinger in an underslip and hold-up stockings, as she appears in the most daring scenes of *Nine and a Half Weeks*. Today models have replaced movie stars as the new repositories of male desire and the fantasy projection of femininity. Have Eva Herzigova and Adriana Sklenaricova replaced Marilyn Monroe and Elizabeth Taylor? Not completely, not if Dolce & Gabbana chose Monica Bellucci for advertising their lingerie. Perhaps the perfect union of glamor and seduction is to be found in the Mediterranean beauty of a former top model who has become an actress.

117 Leading role actresses in Forties and Fifties musicals, Carol Channing and Ginger Rogers are pictured in a scene from the film *The First Traveling Saleslady* in 1956.

120 Ginger Rogers pictured in an underslip in the early 1930's, when she became a leading role actress with her partner Fred Astaire in many famous musicals.

121 A beautiful 1920s star of the silent screen known as the "Golden Dragonfly," Mae Murray, wore underslips and negligees decorated with ribbons and lace.

122-123 Phyllis Haver, the brilliant actress of numerous Hollywood comedies, reveals her sensuality in this intense portrait of 1927.

124-125 The character of Scarlett, the protagonist in *Gone with the Wind*, is one of the most loved in the whole history of cinema. Here Vivien Leigh is pictured in a famous scene from Victor Fleming's film, while her "Mammy" tightens her corset.

AVA GARDNER

Considered the most beautiful actress of her time, Ava is photographed with a silk and lace nightdress and a sensual basque in which she appears in *The little Hut*, directed by Mark Ronson.

Rita Hayworth

This famous American actress – a buxom temptress who went down in the history of cinema as Gilda – wears a refined silk and lace negligee.

Marilyn Monroe

Marilyn Monroe filming on the set of *The Seven Year Itch*, where she playfully takes on the role of the bold yet ingenuous sex symbol.

The simplicity of a black lace set highlights Carroll Baker's beauty in this photograph of 1956, the year in which she starred in *Baby Doll*, the film which made her famous.

ELIZABETH TAYLOR

The famous violet-eyed actress filming a scene from the 1958 drama *Cat on a Hot Tin Roof*. She is intense and passionate as one of the main characters, playing opposite Paul Newman.

JOAN COLLINS

A lace bodysuit and an attitude that's simultaneously coy and innocent: Joan is a timeless sex symbol.

Jane Fonda

In a black satin and lace corset which highlights her perfect "curves," the lovely Jane became famous in the Sixties with the film *Barbarella*, directed by Roger Vadim.

SOPHIA LOREN

The striptease scene from the 1963 film *Yesterday, Today and Tomorrow*, is a favorite among the films of the most famous Italian actress of all time.

Brigitte Bardot

In the Fifities, as the incarnation of a French woman's sensuality, BB represented a myth of freedom from prejudice and femininity. In this picture she is wearing a black corset.

146-147 A series of images which capture the forbidden beauty of Marianne Faithfull, the outrageous representative of 1960s "Swinging London."

148-149 Anita Eckberg, photographed a few years before her role in *La Dolce Vita*, the Fellini masterpiece that made her an icon.

150 Having burst onto the scene in the Sixties, Raquel Welch is still one of the most desirable women in the world. Here she is in *Bedazzled* (1967).

151 Wearing an "innocent" baby doll, the beautiful Julie Christie in a picture from the Sixtie.

As an unsuspected thief in Penelope, *Natalie Wood seems a very long way away from the model student.*

BARBRA STREISAND

Wearing a decidedly unusual item of lingerie in *The Owl and the Pussycat*, Barbra Streisand plays a prostitute who falls in love with an unsuccessful novelist.

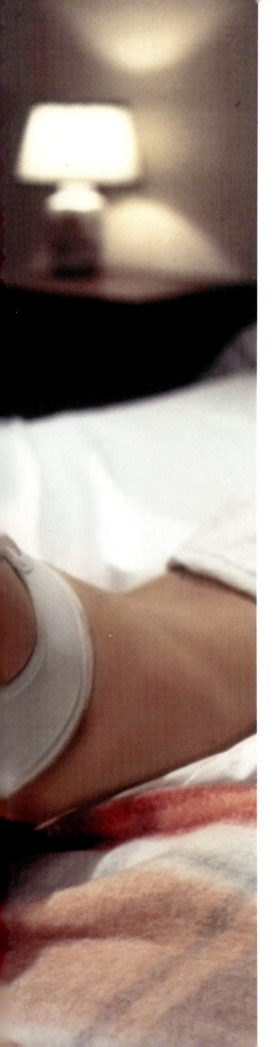

Catherine Deneuve

In 1967, the fascinating and sensual Catherine Deneuve became famous all over the world for her role as Séverine in *Belle de Jour*.

SHARON TATE

Sharon Tate, the unfortunate American actress who was married to Roman Polanski, became a famous fashion magazine cover girl in the 1960s.

Annie Lennox

Aggressive and transgressive, the female "voice" of the Eurythmics knows how to win over an audience with her androgynous beauty.

KIM BASINGER

After *9 ½ weeks* the blond American actress became the erotic obsession of millions of admirers.

MADONNA

The celebrated pop star wore a special bustier by Jean-Paul Gaultier during the Blonde Ambition tour in 1990. From that moment on the pointed bra became a fashion item, and wearing lingerie as a costume became a female pop performance standard.

Kate Moss

In 1994, a very young Kate Moss confidently walks onto fashion photography sets for the first time.

Drew Barrymore

The beautiful Drew, who flaunted a five-star body in *Batman Forever* in 1995, has the face of an angel and the body of a pin-up girl.

CHRISTINA AGUILERA

At the Grammy Awards, on 27 February 2002, the blond American singer and song writer sang "Lady Marmalade," from the film *Moulin Rouge*.

Demi Moore

Returning to film after a six-year absence, the beautiful Demi shows off her enviable physique in *Charlie's Angels: Full Throttle*, where she plays a former angel turned criminal.

Sharon Stone
Halle Berry

Lace underslip and brief leather costume: in the comparison between Sharon Stone and Halle Berry pictured in a scene from *Catwoman*, underwear takes the leading role.

BRITNEY SPEARS

November 2003, two moments in the performance of the "Queen of Pop" at the Shrine Auditorium in Los Angeles for the Annual American Music Awards.

ANGELINA JOLIE

All black for her famous consort Brad Pitt, to suit a real killer. This is in fact the role played by Angelina in the film *Mr. & Mrs. Smith*.

MELANIE GRIFFITH

An unusual black wig for the blond American actress who, in *Something Wild* in 1986, plays a black comedy role.

NOELIA

At Hollywood's Kodak Theater, a passionate interpretation by the Puerto Rican singer who became famous with the hit Candela.

180 An innocent expression and a provocative appearance become a combination charged with great emotional power in Scarlett Johansson, who plays the leading role in *Black Dahlia*.

181 In the most recent version of the film *King Kong*, the giant gorilla loses his life and freedom out of love for the fragile beauty of Naomi Watts.

Monica Bellucci

The beautiful Italian actress Monica Bellucci, a sexy icon of Mediterranean femininity, who moved to France, has migrated successfully from the catwalk to the silver screen.

184-185 The pinup of ivory-skinned Dita Von Tees is on exhibit at the Las Vegas burlesque show that made her famous.

183

Angels on the Catwalk

Angels on the Catwalk

Try and imagine a bra worth 4 million. It is worn like a jewel and indeed it really is a very precious jewel: 3900 precious stones, among which thousands of sparkling black diamonds, 34 rubies and two extremely rare tear-drop-shaped diamonds. Modeled by Brazilian Adriana Lima, it is truly breathtaking.

And who, other than Victoria's Secret, the most famous producer of lingerie in the world, could have created this ultimate marvel? The very famous American lingerie company has created its winning offerings out of provocation and sensationalism.

Victoria's Secret had already demonstrated its desire to shock with its "Red Hot Fantasy," a combo (so to speak) which, for the Festive Season, offered its customers the finest red satin studded with rubies and cascades of hand-cut diamonds. Price? $15 million. No wonder it won a place in the *Guinness Book of Records*. But do not think that Victoria's Secret customers are all Arab sheikhs. This exclusive series of jeweled garments is part of a deliberate marketing strategy, studied to attract millions of "normal" customers.

Just like famous fashion shows, for which the public looks forward to in anticipation like real international events, and which attract the attention of the media worldwide.

In the days leading up to the fashion show, newspapers, posters, television advertisements announce the fashion show as something exceptional that cannot on any account be missed.

Victoria's Secret never disappoints: dazzling floodlights, incredible light displays, extraordinary set design, models who look like beautiful angels who have fallen from heaven. And perhaps an "unforeseen event" (who knows, perhaps contrived?) like that of the animal rights supporter who, at a recent fashion show, managed to elude security and assail Gisele Bündchen who, at that very moment, was advancing along the catwalk in an elephant skin combo.

Result: the television companies from all over the world transmitted the event and the "Victoria's Secret" brand appeared everywhere. Each time the mind of Les Wexner, the creator of the brand, plans new initiatives, the results are always above all expectations.

In 1999, when the fashion show appeared for the first time online to let as many potential customers as possible participate, there were 500 million online visitors in ten weeks, an unexpected success which played havoc with the provider's systems.

The decision to have the most beautiful models in the world wear Victoria's Secret lingerie was equally successful: from Gisele Bündchen to Naomi Campbell, from Laetitia Casta to Eva Herzigova, to Adriana Lima. It is they who make millions of women dream that they can then buy the object of their dreams in more than nine hundred sales outlets (for now only in America), or online (www.victoriassecret.com).

The vast selection of products is another characteristic of the brand.

From lingerie, the company moved on to cosmetics, to bed linens and to ready-to-wear fashion. The message is simple and perfectly on target: it is enough to wear a bra, or a basque, or a romantic slip to feel part of that magical phenomenon of charm and glamor which has become synonymous with Victoria's Secret.

Camus said: "Women are the nearest thing to Heaven on Earth."
Woody Allen

> I dreamed of becoming so beautiful that people would turn around to watch me passing.
>
> — Marilyn Monroe

Men who do not make advances to women are apt to become victims to women who make advances to them.

Walter Bagehot

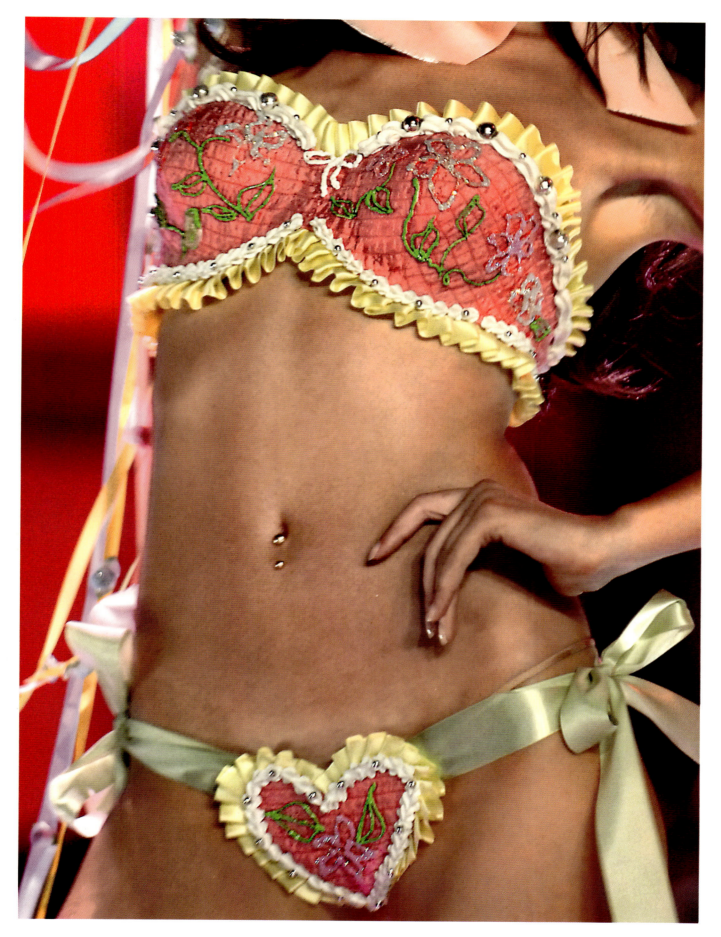

Moderation is a fatal thing.
Nothing succeeds like excess.

Oscar Wilde

Eroticism has reasons which reason does not know.

Nancy Friday

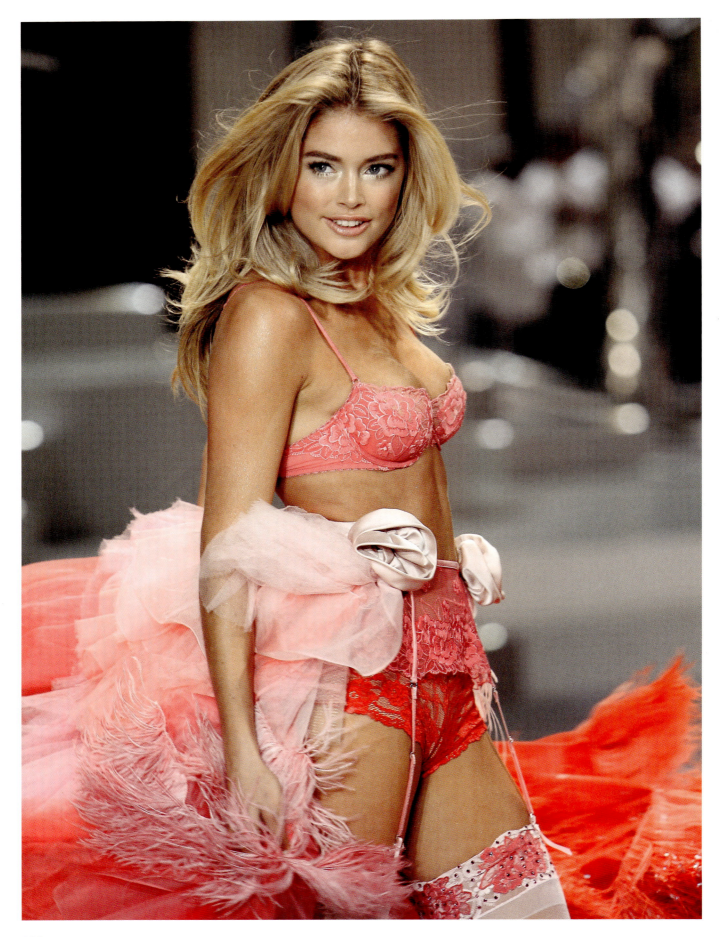

> It's so fascinating to be a woman. It's an adventure that takes such courage; an endless challenge.
> — Oriana Fallaci

Should know her again amongst a thousand, . . . she had . . . a peculiar and graceful carriage of the head. — Thomas De Quincey

Give women the right opportunities and women will be able to do everything. — Oscar Wilde

What would men be without women? Scarce, sir...mighty scarce.

Mark Twain

Photo credits

20th Century Fox Film Corp/Everett Collection/Contrasto: page 176

The Advertising Archives: pages 78, 89, 90, 91, 96, 97, 99, 101, 102-103, 104, 105, 106, 107, 108-109, 112-113

AFP/Getty Images: page 253

Album/Contrasto: pages 134-135

AP/LaPresse: pages 192, 193, 201, 219, 233, 243

Archives du 7eme Art /Photos12.com: pages 136-137, 138, 142, 143, 148-149, 157, 180, 181

Eugene Atget/George Eastman House/Getty Images: page 19

Mario Azuoni/Reuters/Contrasto: pages 207, 212, 213, 220, 223, 224, 225

Bryan Bedder/Getty Images: pages 189, 202, 208, 209, 210, 211

Bettmann/Corbis: page 133

Gregorio Binuya/Everett Collection/Contrasto: pages 194, 195, 206

The Bridgeman Art Library/Archivi Alinari, Firenze: pages 56-57

The Bridgeman Art Library/Getty Images: page 72

Gareth Cattermole/Getty Images: pages 110-111

Collection Cinéma/Photos12.com: pages 160, 172-173

Collection Gregoire/Rue des Archives: pages 92, 93

Corbis: page 158

Culver Pictures/The Art Archive: pages 20, 21

Gianni Dagli Orti/Corbis: pages 64, 70-71

Alexis Duclos/Gamma/Contrasto: page 1

Rainer Eggers/zefa/Corbis: page 48

Mary Evans Picture Library: pages 53, 74, 75, 76, 77, 79, 80, 81, 83

Mary Evans Picture Library/Alamy: page 61

Everett Collection/Contrasto: pages 117, 120, 122-123, 151, 152, 153, 195, 182-183

Mike Fanous/Gamma/Contrasto: pages 216-217, 218

Lake County Museum/Corbis: pages 84-85

Frazer Harrison/Getty Images: page 178

Dave Hogan/Getty Images: page 169

Horst P. Horst / Art + Commerce: page 15

Hulton-Deutsch Collection/Corbis: pages 4-5

Lucas Jackson/Reuters/Contrasto: page 250

Dimitrios Kambouris/Getty Images: page 240

John Kobal Foundation/Getty Images: page 121

The Kobal Collection: pages 130-131, 150

Interfoto/Archivi Alinari, Firenze: page 145

Hervé Lewandowski/Photo RMN: page 68

Mark Mainz/Getty Images: pages 198, 214, 215

Bruno Marzi: page 162

Liz McAulay/Getty Images: pages 38-39

Scott McDermott/Corbis: pages 199, 205

Frank Micelotta/Getty Images: pages 8, 174, 175, 230, 231, 248

Darren Michaels/Columbia/The Kobal Collection: page 171

MGM/The Kobal Collection: page 126

Museum of London/TopFoto/ICP: pages 30, 31

Neil Preston/Corbis: page 163

Shannon Stapleton/Reuters/Contrasto: page 200

MGM Studios/Getty Images: pages 124-125

Terry O'Neill/Hulton Archive/Getty Images: pages 146-147

Paris Film/Five Film/The Kobal Collection: pages 154-155

Rue des Archives: pages 7, 73, 86, 94, 95

Silver Screen Collection/Hulton Archive/Getty Images: page 141

Don Smetzer/Orion/The Kobal Collection: page 177

Swim Ink2, LLC/Corbis: page 65

Alexander Tamargo/Getty Images: pages 226, 227, 228, 228, 232, 234, 235, 236, 237, 239, 242, 247, 249

Amoret Tanner/Alamy: pages 58, 59

Bob Thomas/Popperfoto/Getty Images: page 60

Transcendental Graphics/Getty Images: pages 62-63

Frederique Veysset/Sygma/Corbis: page 165

V&A Images/Victoria and Albert Museum, Londra/Foto Scala, Firenze:
pages 25, 27, 28-29, 32, 34, 35, 36, 37, 40, 42, 43, 44, 47

Roger Viollet/Archivi Alinari, Firenze: pages 66-67, 129

Victor Virgile/Gamma/Contrasto: page 196

Warner Bros/Dc Comics/Album/Contrasto: page 166

WireImage/Getty Images: pages 184-185, 244, 245, 251

WHITE STAR PUBLISHERS

WS White Star Publishers® is a registered trademark
property of Edizioni White Star s.r.l.

© 2010 Edizioni White Star s.r.l.
Via Candido Sassone, 24
13100 Vercelli, Italy
www.whitestar.it

Translation: Catherine Howard
Editing: Peter Skinner

All rights reserved. No part of this publication may be reproduced, stored in a retrieval system
or transmitted in any form or by any means, electronic, mechanical, photocopying,
recording or otherwise, without written permission from the publisher.

ISBN 978-88-544-0477-9

1 2 3 4 5 6   14 13 12 11 10

Stampato in Thailand